The Life, Travels, Labors, and Helpers

of

# Mrs. Amanda Smith

The Famous Negro Missionary
Evangelist

by
Rev. Marshall W. Taylor D. D.

*First Fruits Press*
*Wilmore,*
*Kentucky*
*c2018*

*The life, travels, labors, and helpers of Mrs. Amanda Smith: the famous Negro missionary.*
By Marshall W. Taylor; with an introduction by Rev. J. Krehbiel.
First Fruits Press, © 2018

ISBN: 9781621718499 (print), 9781621718505 (digital), 9781621718512 (kindle)

Digital version at
https://place.asburyseminary.edu/firstfruitsheritagematerial/158/

For all other uses, contact:
First Fruits Press
B.L. Fisher Library
Asbury Theological Seminary
204 N. Lexington Ave.
Wilmore, KY 40390
http://place.asburyseminary.edu/firstfruits

Taylor, Marshall W. (Marshall William), 1846-1887.
  *The life, travels, labors, and helpers of Mrs. Amanda Smith: the famous Negro missionary evangelist* / by Marshall W. Taylor; with an introduction by Rev. J. Krehbiel. – Wilmore, KY: First Fruits Press, ©2018.
    71 pages; cm.
    Reprint. Previously published: Cincinnati: Printed by Cranston & Stowe for the author, 1887, ©1886.
    ISBN: 9781621718499 (pbk.)
    1. Smith, Amanda, 1837-1915.  2. African American women evangelists -- Biography.  3. African American missionaries – Biography.    I. Title.

BV3785.S56 T3 2018

Cover design by Jon Ramsay

asburyseminary.edu
800.2ASBURY
204 North Lexington Avenue
Wilmore, Kentucky 40390

*First Fruits*
THE ACADEMIC OPEN PRESS OF ASBURY SEMINARY

First Fruits Press
*The Academic Open Press of Asbury Theological Seminary*
204 N. Lexington Ave., Wilmore, KY 40390
859-858-2236
first.fruits@asburyseminary.edu
asbury.to/firstfruits

MRS. AMANDA SMITH,

June 2, 1886.

CAPE PALMAS, LIBERIA, WEST COAST OF AFRICA.

THE

# LIFE, TRAVELS, LABORS, AND HELPERS

OF

# MRS. AMANDA SMITH,

THE FAMOUS NEGRO MISSIONARY EVANGELIST.

BY

## REV. MARSHALL W. TAYLOR, D. D.,

AUTHOR OF THE

"UNIVERSAL REIGN OF JESUS;" "LIFE OF DOWNING, THE NEGRO
EVANGELIST;" "PLANTATION MELODIES," ETC., AND EDITOR
OF THE "SOUTHWESTERN CHRISTIAN ADVOCATE."

WITH

## An Introduction by Rev. J. Krehbiel, D. D.,

*Assistant Editor of the "Christian Apologist."*

CINCINNATI:
PRINTED BY CRANSTON & STOWE FOR THE AUTHOR.
1887.

# PREFACE.

THE matter contained in this book was originally designed to be used as an article in the SOUTHWESTERN CHRISTIAN ADVOCATE. But upon examination it proved to be too important for condensation, and too long for use as at first designed without it. Therefore it was determined to give it to the public in the manner here presented, believing that it will fully repay the reader both in interest and profit.

The writer has no apology to make for writing and offering to public patronage another book from his pen, except the belief and desire that it may do good. We are in need of greater enlightenment as to the movements of colored people in public life.

The present is an occasion when Africa and the

African engrosses public thought. The person of whom he writes has, by blood, residence, and labor, much to do with both that country and its people.

We regard the merit of the subject as a sufficient apology. Our chief purpose in writing is with a view of preserving her memory, and placing the example of Sister Smith within the reach of women, especially Negro, and more especially young women, of our day and country.

It can not fail to inspire such as read it; and so, in the light of this noble record, we hope to aid in making many like it.

Such a work is due to Sister Smith merely upon the score of merit alone, and also as a testimonial to many generous-hearted people of the white race and of all Christian creeds, who instructed, advised, and aided her in search for freedom, temporal and spiritual. That this testimonial to the correctness of their views, and the practicalness of their philanthropy, as an illustration of their successful effort at woman building, should be recorded will be admitted.

Upon whom should the delightful labor of making this record more appropriately fall than on him who, like Sister Smith, is a creature of loving philanthropy, largely derived from the same race whence her help has come? The generous patronage which has been extended, and the consideration given to former efforts, assures the writer of forbearance with the many faults abounding in this, and begets within him a reasonable hope that its circulation will be equal to the merit of Sister Smith and his own good intentions in printing this book.

MARSHALL W. TAYLOR.

RICHARDS'S METHODIST EPISCOPAL PARSONAGE,
TROY, MIAMI COUNTY, OHIO, Aug. 23, 1886.

# CONTENTS.

- - - - -

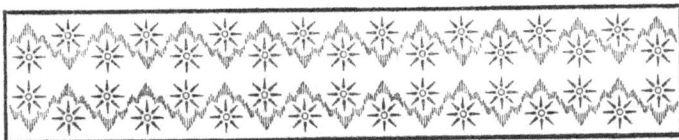

# INTRODUCTION.

AMONG the "elect ladies" of Methodism stands and will stand the name of Amanda Smith. The writer first made her acquaintance at a National Association camp-meeting, at Urbana, as co-worker with John S. Inskip, of blessed memory, Wm. McDonald, and other leaders and workers in the holiness movement. Among the hallowed memories of that meeting, so richly owned of God in the salvation of sinners and the sanctifition of believers, none are so vivid as the part Amanda Smith took in those exercises. Subsequently a nearer acquaintance with her was formed on several occasions, at the Cincinnati Camp-grounds, near Loveland, O. And such nearer acquaintance, and the privilege of sitting under her ministrations, only tended to strengthen the impressions first made.

Sister Amanda Smith is a monument of God's
wondrous grace, a polished shaft in his quiver,
his image "carved in ebony." It was God's
good providence that led her to England, then
to India, and from there to Africa, to labor for
Christ among her own race. As never before,
"Ethiopia is stretching out her hands to God,"
and Amanda Smith will prove an efficient co-
worker with good Bishop Taylor and his devoted
band in leading the millions of the "dark continent" to a knowledge of salvation through our
Lord Jesus Christ.

In the preparation of this sketch of the life
and labors of this saintly woman, Dr. Taylor has
done the Church and the world a service which
can not fail to be appreciated by Christian read-
ers of every name into whose hands this little
book may fall. Such a life as that portrayed
here is a benediction and an inspiration. The
only regret of those who will read these pages
will be that the narrative is not more extended.
Almost every sentence is a gem; and there is
little, if any thing, that one could wish had been
left unsaid. The experience here told will lead
others to a renewed consecration of heart and

life to the Master's service. It will help to
quicken the missionary spirit, and thus hasten
the coming of the kingdom of God. It will
tend to break down the prejudice of race, and
hasten the glad day when a man or woman shall
be judged, not by the color of the skin, but by
the quality of mind and heart.

The writer well remembers the feeling of in-
dignation that stirred his inmost soul some years
ago when, sitting one beautiful Sabbath morning
in one of the fashionable Methodist churches in
an Eastern city, he saw Amanda Smith met at
the door by the sexton and told to go into the
*gallery.* True, the seats in that gallery were as
comfortable and the surroundings as luxurious as
in the main audience room, and the writer had
of his own choice taken a seat there; but why
should this woman, whose preference was for a
seat in the main audience room, be shown into
the gallery? The color of her skin was the
only reason. At that very time she would have
received a glad welcome in hundreds of Christian homes in Cincinnati, and been made more
than welcome in the Methodist pulpits of that
city. But no matter; such as she can well take

such slights with all Christian meekness, and by the purity of their lives and their labors for God and humanity compel recognition of their worth.

Amanda Smith's labors, which have been so signally owned of God among all classes in this country, in England, in India and Africa, will without doubt continue to abound until her work is done, and she shall receive the plaudit of, " Well done, good and faithful servant; enter thou into the joy of thy Lord."

J. KREHBIEL.

# MRS. AMANDA SMITH.

## HER PARENTAGE AND BIRTH.

AMANDA was one of a family of thirteen children. She was the daughter of Mr. Samuel Berry, a slave of Mr. Darby Insace. He married Mariam Mathews, a born slave of Doctor Shadrach Green, at Long Green, Maryland. Mr. Berry bought himself, his wife, and the freedom of five of his children. Of the five children whose freedom he bought, two are now living—his eldest boy, William Talbot, and the subject of this narrative. The eight who remained in slavery are supposed to have died before freedom. If any are now alive their whereabouts is unknown to the writer.

Amanda Berry was born March 17, in 1836, according to her best information, at Long Green, Maryland. Among her earliest recollections is the kind face and gentle voice of her grandmother, who, she remembers hearing, was mar-

ried three times. Her first husband's name was
Mathews, and the last, Burgess. The name of
the second is not remembered. They lived near
Monkton, in the State of Maryland, and there
her grandmother died. Her father died in Philadelphia, July, 1868, and her mother at York,
Pennsylvania; but the year we do not know.

The deed of Mr. Berry's and his family's freedom is recorded in the Baltimore Court-house.
He had a copy of it, with the county seal attached, in due form, which he often showed to
his children; but his copy was lost after his death.

Her grandmother, father, and mother were all
truly pious people. Her grandmother was mighty
in prayer, and her mother and father often said
that to her grandmother's prayers they owed their
freedom. Her mother, inheriting the spirit of her
grandmother, was a woman of great faith and
strong moral courage. And this faith and courage, in the third generation, has given to the
world Amanda Smith.

Her mother's young mistress was converted in
answer to prayer, after the old-fashioned style, at
a camp-meeting. This greatly disturbed the family, who were staunch Presbyterians, after the
strictest type, and did not believe in noise. But·
the young lady could not keep still. Her fervent religious life, however, was of but short

duration. She had only a few months' enjoyment of her new-found treasure, then the Lord called her to himself. Every creature comfort was ministered to her, but the heavenly call could not be stayed. When nearing her last moments she called the family about her dying bed, and said, "I want you to promise me that you will let Samuel have Mariam and the children"— meaning the parents and brothers and sisters of her about whom we have written. Of course it was a great shock, for they were little expecting such a request. It was not readily granted; but for three days, though weakened by a preying disease and nearing death, she earnestly pressed the same request. At last she was told her desire should be granted.

A few hours later she asked "Aunt Mariam," as she had always called our subject's mother, who had been her nurse from childhood, to sing for her a favorite hymn. "Aunt Mariam" began in that clear, weird, unique, but, to the descendants of Africa, peculiar and melodious tone; her voice rose higher, filled with tender pathos, broken now and then by emotion. It was an enchanting moment. The young lady folded her arms, bade all good-bye, and while the sweet song was still sounding in her soul she was gathered home unto the Lord.

Mrs. Mariam Berry, the mother of our subject, had been converted about two years before the death of her young mistress, just related. Verily,

> "God moves in a mysterious way,
> His wonders to perform."

The promise made to the dying young lady by her family was faithfully kept, and strictly fulfilled. Therefore Samuel Berry was permitted to buy himself and five children, among them Amanda, as we have said. Does not the reader, with the writer, fervently say, "Thank the Lord?" And is it not clear enough that, in this case at least, Ethiopia hath effectually stretched forth her hands to God, and a princess truly come forth out of Egypt? Human slavery is a great curse; but through it is more clearly revealed the saving power of the Gospel and the precious influence of Christianity in the case we have cited.

## CHILDHOOD AND YOUTH.

From her earliest recollection Amanda had religious impressions and desires. She never went to any colored school, and her scholastic advantages were not extensive, nor could she to this day properly be called a woman of literary culture. But if both could not be had, she has that which is far

better: thorough moral culture. She was not entirely bereft of opportunities to learn from books,
however. Her father and mother were both able
to read, her father being the better reader of the
two. He spent a part of every Sunday in reading the Bible to his children. Amanda always
prayed to be good, like her mother; and the spirit
of that mother has doubtless come upon her, endowed with grace equal to the superior demands
of the times in which she lives and labors.

She first went to school at the age of eight
years. Her teacher was a very earnest Christian
white lady, Miss Isabella Dill by name. The
father of Miss Dill was an old-fashioned Methodist preacher, a very holy man. The teachings
of her home Miss Dill brought to her pupils at
school. She seemed to be especially interested in
Mrs. Berry and Amanda, and Amanda was fondly
attached to her. The school was held in an un-
occupied house just opposite the place where
Samuel Berry, his wife, and children lived. It
was in the country between Newmarket and
Strausburg, on the Baltimore and York turn-
pike, in York County, Pennsylvania. Here she
met with the difficulty which usually presents
itself to Negro children when attending mixed
schools. She says, "Sometimes I would be greatly
disturbed in my religious devotions by the chil-

dren calling me 'nigger,' and at other times by
various forms of unkind treatment from them.
*Then old prejudices* would rise, and for a season
I would cease to pray."

Her next teacher was Doctor Joseph Hendricks, a white man, who taught at a place called
"Rule's School-house," two miles from the place
where she first attended school. It was a Winter
term of three months; but our subject did not
continue in school the entire term, as her whole
time in school together does not exceed ninety
school days.

After leaving Doctor Hendricks's school, she
next attended one taught by Mr. Walter Murray,
who proved to be a kind, affectionate teacher,
taking great interest in her, as well as in the
other Negro children who attended the school,
which does not seem to have been the case with
Doctor Hendricks. There were four Negro children in the school, but they did not remain
very long.

About this time Mr. Berry went to live near
Strausburg, where he was better acquainted, and
where he supposed his opportunities for making
a living would improve.

The gentle reader will not suppose that a man
with a wife and five children, whose ransom, with
his own, he had paid in gold earned by his own

unaided efforts by night, before day, and on Sundays, had within the first ten years of freedom found much leisure or opportunity to enjoy the poetic luxuries of life. The reverse is true.

Samuel Berry found it quite as much as he could do, with increasing years and waning strength, to make both ends meet at Christmas time. It finally became necessary for all hands of the family who could to join and help him with his burden. The call of duty was plain. Amanda must choose between the school-room and a place at service. Her decision was quickly reached, and she went to live with Mrs. Latimer, a Southern lady, whose native place was Savannah, Georgia.

During this time there was a great revival in that place; indeed, a revival was sweeping over all the country. The people were stirred, and every one seemed to be deeply concerned. There were no Negro Churches anywhere in that part of the country; but the Lutheran, Albright, and Methodist Episcopal Churches each had white congregations there.

## EXPERIENCE AS A MEMBER OF A MIXED CONGREGATION, AND THE RESULT.

She frequently attended the Methodist Episcopal Church, finally became deeply interested in its services, and, being thoroughly satisfied with her religious experience, she at last united with it. In speaking of her experience while a member of this Church, Sister Smith says: "I do not remember the name of the minister, but my class-leader's name was Ludril. He had a grand pair of lungs, and was a good leader. I was the only colored person in the Church at the time I joined, and it became customary to leave me till the last in every thing—communion, or what not. So I was always the last one to speak in class. Sometimes the class would be very full. It convened immediately after morning preaching; and I had to go home to get dinner, so the children could go to Sunday-school. The delay in leading me often belated me with my work. Then I would get a scolding; so it did me but little good to stay for class. I used to *wish* I was white, so I could be led in turn. If I sat on the first end of the seat, the leader would commence leading at the far end of it; and if I sat between two white sisters, then he would lead them and leave me. So, to retain my situation with Mrs. Latimer, I had to quit going to class."

The reader may infer from this experience of Sister Berry that contact of white people and Negroes in the same schools or congregations by no means equals social intercourse. That is true;

but social equality does not depend upon, it is entirely independent of, social contact and connection. The truth is, that Negro congregations and schools in the same organizations with the whites, under the same supervisions, doctrines, and rules, afford superior opportunities for the cultivation of Negro piety, talent, and usefulness.

About the time Sister Berry left off attending class her father moved to York, Pennsylvania. In this town she for the first time had the privilege of attending service with a colored congregation. Her race pride was flattered, her sense was humored; but, in sober truth, her stock of grace was well-nigh exhausted. Amanda Berry had backslidden. The attempted congregational mingling had proven disastrous to a growth in grace. She remained in this condition until March 17, 1856.

She still retains her membership with the African Methodist Episcopal Church.

## SOJOURNING AMONG THE FRIENDS.

The sweet, mild manner, unadorned costume, sturdy integrity, deep piety, and all-embracing philanthropy characteristic of the Friends, had charms for Sister Berry. So, about March, 1856, she went to reside with a family of Friends at Columbia, Pennsylvania, Robert Mifflin being the head of the family. Here the situation was conducive to piety. She returned to the Lord; and after struggling in ignorance, darkness, and doubt for three months, it pleased the Lord to scatter the darkness of unbelief and set her soul at liberty. Speaking of that occurrence, Sister Smith says: "Oh, what joy and *real peace* swept through my soul like a flood of light and love! I obtained a *clear* and *distinct* witness of the Spirit that God for Christ's sake had pardoned all my sins. And though I have had many storms and conflicts from Satan, yet, glory to God! I have never had a doubt from that hour. From then until this time I have had no spiritual trouble."

Although Sister Smith retains her membership in the African Methodist Episcopal Church, it was among the members and ministers of others, chiefly the Methodist Episcopal Church, where she obtained the true Gospel light, and that Christian fellowship which, preparing her for her world-wide parish, placed and maintained her in the performance of its continuous and heaven-honored duties.

Sister Smith's convictions are deep and abiding that "he who feareth is not yet made perfect in love," and that "perfect love casteth out fear." She is satisfied with the work she is doing, and with that part of the field which she is gleaning;

but if the Lord leads the way she is ready at his call to recross the ocean and again declare his saving help to the people of her native land.

## MARRIED—THE HIGHER LIFE.

Mrs. Smith has been twice married, and is the mother of five children. The name of her first husband was Calvin M. Devine, of Columbia, Pennsylvania. He died in July, 1856. She next married Rev. James H. Smith, of Philadelphia, Pennsylvania, a local deacon in the African Methodist Episcopal Church. Mr. Smith died November, 1869, in the State of New York, since which time Mrs. Smith has been a widow. Of her five children, only one daughter survives, who now resides in Baltimore, Maryland.

Shortly after her conversion, by reading the Bible and praying much in secret, Mrs. Smith was awakened to feel the need of personal holiness. And on this point she says: "Not hearing the doctrine of holiness definitely preached or taught, though I believe there were many of the older brethren and sisters in the Church who enjoyed this experience, I was much confused in my mind, and hence blundered along in the darkness, not knowing that this blessed grace, like justification, was received by faith in Christ alone."

She finally made a full and unconditional surrender to God; and on the first Sunday in September, 1868, in old Green Street Methodist Episcopal Church, New York, while the sainted John S. Inskip was pastor, during a sermon which he was preaching from the text, "Put ye on the new man, which after God is created in righteousness and true holiness," it pleased God to bestow upon her the blessing of perfect love.

Relating this experience, Sister Smith says: "As he went on explaining the truth, it pleased the Lord to send the Holy Ghost upon me in great power, assuring me there and then that my prayer for a clean heart was heard, and that God himself had sent the answer. *Glory to the Holy Trinity!*"

From that hour Mrs. Smith has never doubted the power and purpose of God, not only to justify, but also wholly to sanctify and keep the soul stayed on him in this life.

Mrs. Smith's experience was that mixed congregations, between black and white people, was a fruitful source of inconvenience and spiritual vexation to her, growing out of the slights and neglects to which she was subjected by the perfunctory and indifferent manner in which officials performed their duty toward her, as in the case of Brother Ludril, the class-leader above referred to. But the fact that she could sit in the same seat with, and at her option between, two white sisters, tends to show that in the congregation itself there was a fair degree of social toleration, if not positive social intercourse with her; so that, after all, the practice of the people, even there and at that time, was not in full harmony with the conduct of the leader. And in Green Street Church she finds such congenial surroundings as tend to promote her search for perfect love, although in a white congregation and under the ministry of a white preacher, and since her connection with a Negro congregation failed, through its ministry, to aid her efforts to reach the fair plains of a higher Christian life.

The further lesson of this experience is that Negro congregations, in such organic connection with the white people as to secure the greatest social advancement on the one hand, combined with the higher moral and religious culture of the whites on the other, is the most conducive means to Christian cultivation among the blacks as an end.

And precisely such are the facilities enjoyed by the Negro members of the Methodist Episcopal Church. This phase of the subject is worthy of very especial consideration from the reader.

## IN PUBLIC LIFE.

In a brief time after receiving the great blessing of entire sanctification the Spirit of the Lord led Sister Smith out into public work. She was called to preach—there was no doubt of that; she could not confer with flesh and blood—she was sure of that; but yet she needed the warrant of the Church and the influence and prestige of Christian authority at her back. But the Church did not give licence to women to preach. Here was a sad dilemma. She was a child of Providence. Providence could open the way. The work was the Lord's, and so was the power. She could

> "Judge not the Lord by feeble sense,
> But trust him for his grace."

Providence did open the way. Rev. Nelson Turpin, at that time pastor of Sullivan Street African Methodist Episcopal Church, New York City, found a way to preserve the order of the Church, while he at the same time loosed Sister Smith and let her go. He gave her a letter of recommendation to any pastor who would be willing to accept her services. But the power of the Lord so manifestly attended and clearly attested the divine approval of Sister Smith's course, that she speedily found more calls for service than she was able to fill, and had little use for the recommendation given her.

Speaking of the matter, Sister Smith says: "The Lord himself took hold of me and sent me out, like Abraham of old, from among my own people, to a strange people and a strange land. I found myself laboring among white people with marvelous success—first at camp-meetings, and later in their different Churches all over the land."

The first meeting held by Sister Smith was at Lynn, near Boston, Massachusetts, in "Old Lynn Common Church," of which Doctor Newhall was then pastor. The meeting lasted ten days, and was quite successful. She then went to East Syracuse, New York; then to Marblehead. At the latter Church Rev. Mr. Bridges was pastor. Then she labored at Rockport, Massachusetts, with Rev. Dr. Derick as pastor. In this meeting the Lord wonderfully poured out his Spirit in the saving of his people. Then she went to Salem, Massachusetts, and labored with Rev. Dr. Daniel Dorchester, pastor of the First Methodist Episcopal Church in that place. Then at Worcester, Massachusetts, she wrought for the Lord with Rev. J. S. Chadwick, pastor there. She then came to Seventeenth Street Church, New York, upon the invitation of Rev. W. H.

Boole, pastor there at that time. After this, in quick succession, she was at the James Street Church, with Rev. Dr. Hamilton, and Doctor Stratton, at Yonkers, New York.

By this time New England and the Middle States were full of her fame, and her name was rapidly extending westward. After a few meetings in Connecticut, she was invited to Park Street Church, in Cincinnati, where Rev. Mr. Meredith was pastor. And then came innumerable invitations to other places. In Ohio, Indiana, Minnesota, Baltimore, and Washington City the demand for service was far greater than her time and strength would allow. In Brooklyn she had calls to Mr. Beecher's Plymouth Church, Dr. Niles's, and Dr. Buddington's, besides the Baptist and Colored Presbyterian Churches of the place. Dr. H. H. Garnett threw open his door, and gave her the right of way. Sixth Avenue Church, New York, and the Friends' Meeting House, in Brooklyn, also sought her services.

In each of these Churches Mrs. Smith conducted meetings from a week to ten days in duration, and her fame became national. She was always ready, never hesitated a moment, and hailed with pleasure every call to assist colored pastors. She says: " But it was all the Lord's work;" for "he had said to me in the outset,

'Behold I set before you an open door, and no man shall shut it.' 'This is the Lord's doings, and it is marvelous in our eyes.'"

## PREPARING FOR FOREIGN LABOR.

In 1879 Mrs. Smith left America, and sailed for England. She was all alone—yet not alone; for the Lord bade her go, and promised to go with her.

While holding a meeting in old Sands Street Church, Brooklyn, she chanced to meet Miss Price, an English lady who was visiting Mrs. Parker, a friend of hers. Mrs. Smith was at the time very much debilitated from overwork. Miss Price observing this, seemingly in a casual manner, remarked to Mrs. Smith that a trip to Europe would be nice and she thought beneficial to her. She said, "I intend to go to Europe in April myself, and I think a trip would do you good." Says Mrs. Smith, "I supposed only well folks went to Europe for a change, but such as me never, no, never."

The matter then passed out of Mrs. Smith's mind and was forgotten; but after a few days Miss Price mentioned it again, when Mrs. Smith replied, "Of gold and silver have I none; but it takes money to go to England." This was precisely what Miss Price knew, and to this point she had been directing her conversation from the first. So she promptly advised Mrs. Smith to take the matter to the Lord in prayer, saying, "And if you decide to go, *I will see that the money is all right.*"

This caused Mrs. Smith to reflect, and it then came to her mind that another good friend of hers, Mrs. Mary C. Johnson, had several months previously expressed a belief that the Lord had work for her to do in Great Britain.

Mrs. Smith did take the matter to God in prayer, and it was clearly revealed to her as according to his will that she should go.

Then came the ties of home, the society of loved ones, the charms of her daughter, congenial spirits in Christian work, the graves of beloved dead, the scenes of early childhood, and the love of country, earnestly pleading against her resolution to follow the leadings of the Spirit which was in her. It was his opportunity, and Satan improved it. He enlarged upon the dangers and magnified the perils of a voyage at sea under any circumstances, and especially to her, a lone woman, in view of the discourtesies to which women of her race were usually subjected in places of public resort and by common carriers. "But the Lord remembereth that we are dust," and in his mercy drew near, strengthening Sister

Smith for this new trial. She says, "I thank God he gave me the victory, so that from my heart I was able to say:

> "'Lord, obediently we'll go,
> Gladly leaving all below;
> Only thou our leader be,
> And we still will follow thee.'"

In about a week after this resolution was formed a letter from Mrs. Mary C. Johnson arrived, and, among other things, contained the following, "Mr. Johnson and I sail for Europe at a given date in May, and will be glad to have you with us." There, now: "Surely God is good to Israel, even to such as are of a clean heart."

This was all the Lord's doings.

There was only one week to prepare for the journey, and Mrs. Smith found it impossible to prepare herself in so short a time. Says Sister Smith, "I took the letter and spread it on a chair, and said, 'Lord, if you will help me I will go alone.' The assurance was given me. I arose and said, 'All right, Lord. I will obey thee. Amen.'"

After a pleasant voyage of ten days from Philadelphia, in the steamer *Ohio*, Captain Morris in command, Sister Smith was landed in Liverpool, England; and in her soul the beautiful lines of William Whiting were doubtless

swelling up in praise and thankfulness to God
for her safe passage over the ocean's perils:

> "Eternal Father! strong to save,
>     Whose arm hath bound the restless wave."

Sister Smith says, "Every step of the way I
could see the hand of the Lord."

She secured first-class passage on the steamer;
this no colored lady had ever done on that
steamer before. At the table she mingled with
other first-class passengers, and could see no difference between the treatment others received and
that extended to her. But it was a new thing,
and she says, "At first some of the passengers
felt badly, and inquired why I did not take a
cheaper rate." The fare was seventy dollars,
which was regarded as a large sum for a colored
lady to pay.

Captain Morris proved to be a finished gentleman in all his bearings. He was at pains to
make Mrs. Smith comfortable in every way. He
begged her to be free, and inform him if at any
time she was treated improperly. Thanking him,
she agreed to do as he had directed; but she had
no occasion to complain, for her treatment was
perfect.

Two Sundays were spent aboard the ship. On
the first they were all pretty well shaken up with

sea-sickness, but by the second Sunday were all fairly recovered. There was no minister aboard, and the captain invited Sister Smith to conduct the services, which she consented to do.

## PREACHING ON THE SEA.

The saloon was arranged, the bell was rung, and at the appointed hour the passengers were invited to the services. All came, perfect order prevailed, and Sister Smith says, "The Lord helped me to *speak*, sing, and pray."

At the close of the meeting they crowded about her on every side. Many salutations of "God bless you!" reached her ears. Some of the very dignified people, who had hardly glanced at her before, now eagerly grasped her hand, and with tears starting from their eyes bade her many, many times, "God bless you!"

There was a Quaker gentleman and son on board the ship, to whose interest and good offices the permission to hold these services was largely attributable. Speaking of him, Sister Smith says, "The Friends have always been straight on the subject of woman's preaching."

Her fellow-passengers, however, were mostly Episcopalians and Presbyterians, to whom the sight of a woman preaching must have possessed the character of a novelty, if not a disorder.

" But the Lord's ways are not our ways, and his doings are wondrous in our eyes." So let it be.

## ON ENGLISH SOIL.

The voyage was otherwise uneventful than as already narrated. The days spent on shipboard were days of close communion with God. A great work for God was just ahead. The coming event cast its shadow before, and the great Negro missionary was in spirit already in the midst of the on-coming revival. Her time alternated between planning for her approaching campaign, and studying God in the vasty deep beneath and around her and the vaster depths of ether above. The Spirit of the Lord came upon her more than ever before, anointing her for her approaching labors.

She proceeded from Liverpool directly to Keswick, where a great holiness convention was then sitting. Here the Rev. Canon Batersby, of St. John's Vicarage, was chairman of the convention. The distinguished prelate, with other Christian gentlemen and ladies in attendance, received Sister Smith with the utmost Christian cordiality. There seemed an utter unconsciousness that her being a Negro made any difference at all. To the pure all things are pure. She was known as a Christian worker, and so received. The Master's English vineyard needed laborers, and she was warmly pressed to enter it everywhere in England, Scotland, and Ireland.

She spent a year and eight months in England, engaged in holding evangelical services at Liverpool, Berkenhead, Leeds, Doncaster, Manchester, Newcastle-on-Tyne, Cambridge, Lester, Plymouth, Darlington, London, and many other places. Then proceeding to Scotland, she found the way opened, and many invitations pressing her, at Perth, Aberdeen, Glasgow, Greenock, Edinburgh, and other points. Some of these she was unable to fill for want of time and strength, especially that at Edinburgh.

In England, as in America, Mrs. Smith found that the Lord was owning the work; that his Church was not opposing, but helping it; that neither color nor sex was a hindrance; and that her chief work was to keep her mind and body in the best state of fitness at all times to follow where and when the Lord directed and opened the way before her.

## ON TO INDIA.

The Lord marvelously opened the way for her to visit India. Miss Lulu Drake, who is now Mrs. W. B. Osborne, of Niagara Falls, had spent some time in India, and having recuperated

by her vacation, was returning to her work in
India. She had known Mrs. Smith in America
years before. They had also met in London.
Mrs. Smith was now beginning to think the
Lord had something for her to do in India;
Miss Drake felt the same way; and after a con-
versation with her the impression upon Mrs.
Smith's mind was deepened. She felt sure the
hand of the Lord was revealed in it.

The two ladies placed the matter before the
Lord in prayer, and then waited for his further
guidance. Mrs. Smith says, "I had no money,
only as I trusted the Lord to send what I needed;
neither had I any doubt that he had need of me
in India."

> "His purposes will ripen fast,
> Unfolding every hour."

Miss Drake determined to go overland. This
was more expensive than a trip by sea would
have been. It was now Mrs. Smith's full deter-
mination to go to India. That such was her
duty, both ladies were now convinced. She,
therefore, made up her mind to accompany Miss
Drake on her overland trip.

Speaking of the matter, Mrs. Smith says, "I
asked the Lord to let me go overland also."
She knew the Lord could, and she fully believed
that he would, put it into the hearts of those who

had the means to furnish her with what she needed for the trip. Coupled with her desire to save souls in India, but in a subordinate degree, was the desire to see the many objects of historic interest abounding in that country, of which she had heard and read so much. She believed that the Lord would do all that she desired, and her faith was well founded; for just two days before she was ready to leave London she received every cent needed for her expenses, with a thorough outfit for the journey, and with five pounds ($25) for contingencies.

The arm of the Lord was revealed. Sister Smith understood it, and flew to his secret place, that she might pour out her soul in praises to Him whose mercy endureth forever.

At this time Mrs. Smith's daughter was at school in Baltimore; but her comfort was ever present on the thoughtful mother's heart. Winter was approaching, and the daughter's only source of support was the mother. It was a sufficient source. To supply the wants of her daughter, and secure her continuance at school, Sister Smith had sent three months' board in advance, together with clothing suitable and sufficient for the Winter. This left her very little means for personal use. This daughter and herself Sister Smith had supported by hired service and washing and ironing until the Lord thrust her out into this work. She had ever found him faithful to such as keep his covenant and his testimonies, and had learned more and more to trust and depend implicitly upon him. All this was known to the Lord, and hence the provision so opportunely made by divine direction for the expenses of her journey to India.

The instance above noted is not an isolated one in the career of Mrs. Smith; for she says, with reference to this point: "Since the Lord sanctified my heart, in 1868, and established my faith, I have been living by faith. I have never received a cent from any Church or organization in the whole time. In all of my travels the Lord has supplied all my needs, and I have trusted in him alone. I can say, of a truth, that not one of all his good promises has failed, but that all are being fulfilled. 'Praise the Lord, O my soul, and forget not all his benefits.'"

Mrs. Smith has been made to realize, by substantial and practical testimony, that her friends were many, and resided in many lands. Touching this, she says: "Some of the kind friends that helped me I have never seen. They have heard of the work and of me as an humble instrument in God's hands, and he has moved them to remember me. Praise his Name!"

" We thank thee, O Father,
  For all things bright and good,
The seed-time and the harvest,
  Our life, our health, our food."

## IN THE LAND OF BRAHM AND BUDDHA.

The journey from London to Bombay gave
Mrs. Smith a glance at Egypt, the land where
her forefathers wrought splendidly, and whence
many a grimy monument of theirs peers down
with awe-inspiring ken upon the sweeping centuries. Almost every object was full of interest,
and served to enrich her store of illustrations for
future use.

But at length the journey was ended, and Mrs.
Smith found herself alone in the land where the
religion of Brahm and Buddha had darkened
counsel for many centuries by words without inspiration. Impressed with an awful sense of the
grandeur of her work and the sublimity of the
cause in which she was now about to engage,
she presented herself, and was kindly received by
the Churches in India. The Rev. Mr. Row was
at Bombay, Rev. Dr. Thoburn at Calcutta, Rev.
Mr. Robinson at Rangoon, British Burmah, Dr.
Scott at Bareilly, Dr. Waugh at Lucknow, Rev.
Dennis Osborne at Allahabad, Brother Leonard
at Agra, Rev. N. Cheeney at Nynee Tal, and Rev.

Dr. Johnson at Cawnpore. Sister Smith visited all these Churches, and was invited to many others, which time and space forbid us to mention here.

Her sojourn in India was of nineteen months' duration. Her labors were abundant and fruitful; but she felt herself drawn toward England again, and in July, 1881, returned to that country. The missionaries of India, among them Rev. Dennis Osborne, Babu Ram Chandra Bose, Miss Thoburn, and others, have spoken to the writer in high praise concerning Sister Smith's labors in that country.

## AT THE ECUMENICAL CONFERENCE IN LONDON.

In July, 1881, Sister Smith found herself again in London, and also found London the seat of one of the greatest religious gatherings of the nineteenth century. World-wide Methodism was convening there by its representatives, for the purpose of a great "Ecumenical Conference."

She must attend it, of course. She did so, sitting in City Road Chapel, the site where Methodism was born. And who knows but that the spirit of its great founder inspired her with yet greater missionary zeal, as she there contemplated the culmination of his great planting, after the lapse of a century of years?

For sixty days she lingered in England, and then, fully persuaded that it was her destiny to do so, she sailed from Liverpool to Liberia. The voyage was an uneventful one, and terminated by her safe arrival on the sun-burnt continent.

## IN LIBERIA.

On the 24th of December, 1881, Sister Smith sailed from Liverpool for Liberia, and arrived at Monrovia, west coast of Africa, the 18th of January, 1882. The Lord was with her then, as he had been at other times and in all other lands.

She had her first attack of fever three weeks after landing. During her prostration she was the guest of Miss May Sharp, a zealous and devout missionary then at service in Liberia. She was tenderly cared for, and was speedily restored. The mercy of the Lord was with her, and led her out into his work.

She became the guest of Mrs. Martha Payne, sister-in-law of late President J. S. Payne, who will be remembered as one of the Liberian delegates to the General Conference of the Methodist Episcopal Church in Cincinnati, Ohio, in 1880. She was warmly welcomed and cordially received by the Methodist Episcopal Church in Monrovia. Rev. Charles Pitman, who was Liberian delegate to the General Conference in 1872, in Brooklyn, New York, and Rev. James Deputy were foremost in the extension of kindnesses, because nearest to her; but the members of the Liberian Conference generally displayed the utmost Christian consideration for her, and together with her the Lord poured out his blessing upon them.

Sister Smith says: "They have been as fathers to me, a stranger in a strange land. Praise the Lord! And may he pour out all his blessings upon all the members of the Liberian Annual Conference. I have some sons in the conference whom I desire to see become strong men for God. Pray that they may be filled with the Holy Ghost. Amen."

Brother Robert Deputy, who is pastor of the Presbyterian Church, and brother of Rev. James Deputy, exhibited a most fraternal spirit toward her. He frequently invited her to fill the pulpit of his Church, which she as frequently did, to the edification of its membership. Mr. Gibson, who was pastor of the Protestant Episcopal Church in Liberia at that time, also treated her with distinguished consideration, inviting her to conduct services preparatory to the communion, which she did, the Lord working with her there. She found, also, in Africa, as in other countries, that the ministry and membership of the Baptist denomination, with very rare and unnoteworthy exceptions, were kind and helpful to her in her work. It will be worth while to state that Miss Mary Sharp, of whom Sister Smith has so kindly spoken, is a young white lady, appointed to the Liberian Mission by the Methodist Episcopal Church.

## MEETS BISHOP TAYLOR.

On the 22d of January, 1885, Sister Smith left Monrovia for the purpose of attending the Liberian Conference, which was appointed to meet at Grand Bassa February 5th, and from thence it was her plan to return again to Monrovia. But learning that the bishop had arranged to stop at Cape Palmas, Sister Smith says, "The Spirit of the Lord, I believe, said to me, 'This is your chance.'"

For six months Sister Smith had been all prepared and awaiting an opportunity so visit Cape Palmas. It is not always that one can meet with this opportunity, as there is no regular line of steamers between Monrovia and Cape Palmas. One must keep on the watch for transient boats that will stop at the Cape; and one such chance as this Mrs. Smith had missed, and hence was unable to reach that place, although she had had an appointment with Rev. Charles Harmon, of precious memory, who was at that time serving as pastor on the Cape; but who, just a few weeks before the assembling of his conference and the arrival of Sister Smith, was summoned to the presence of God in heaven. He had a great desire to welcome her, and as a father beloved she still reveres his memory.

After the death of Brother Harmon, Sister Smith supposed herself free from that appointment; but the Lord had ordered otherwise, and on meeting Bishop Taylor she laid the matter before him and asked his advice. Said the bishop, "I think this is just the time for you to go." This was enough. Sister Smith was convinced, and made herself ready for the trip. With reference to it she says, "How very clear it has been to me, since I came to Cape Palmas, that it is the Lord's ordering!"

In company with Bishop Taylor, Sister Smith left Bassa on Tuesday, February 16, and arrived at Cape Palmas Friday, February 19, 1885. Her first impressions, inspired by the hospitality of the people toward the bishop and herself, are expressed with reference to him in these words, "I was delighted with the spirit of kindness shown the bishop on his arrival. Praise the Lord!"

On Friday night Bishop Taylor preached to a crowded Church, and the Lord attended his

words with the power and demonstration of the
Holy Ghost sent down from heaven. On Saturday he held quarterly conference, and at night he
preached again. On Sabbath morning he was
again ready for duty. In speaking of his sermon
and labors in general, Sister Smith says, "O,
what a mine of truth is stirred up in this grand
old hero! What powerful sermons were the
three preached by the bishop in this place!
Many, many hearts fervently said Amen."

But these solemn services were cut short in
the height of their fervent flame and holy ec-
stasy; for, just as they were about to proceed
with the sacrament of the Lord's-supper, word
came that the steamer had called for the bishop,
according to arrangement made by him while in
Liverpool. Much to his regret, he was com-
pelled to leave.

His sudden and unexpected departure occa-
sioned genuine sorrow among the people, and
perhaps most of all among the children; for he
had promised them a lecture in the afternoon.
But this, also, was the Lord's doings. The great
man was gone; but the great woman remained.
Who but she should be his proxy? She was in-
clined to excuse herself; but the people demand
a sacrifice; the Lord was calling. Meekly she
responded, " Here am I; send me, send me."

Sister Smith did the best she could; and if the reader has ever heard her when taken under just such circumstances, then we need not inform him how much there is of solid comfort in the best she can do.

## PREACHING ON THE CAPE.

After the death of Brother Harmon, Rev. Daniel Ware was appointed preacher in charge at Cape Palmas, and Rev. James Deputy was appointed presiding elder of the district. Sister Smith says, "Brother Ware had been very sick for weeks, so that on the following Saturday after my arrival he was obliged to leave the Cape for his home and family in Monrovia."

Brother Ware was detained by his illness two months at home. During his sickness Sister Smith spent some time working in his charge, performing any duties that she could, and modestly speaks of her labors as follows: "I held Bible readings in the church, and endeavored to call the attention of the people definitely to the subject of holiness."

The Lord blessed Sister Smith in her efforts, and many hearts were made whole. Among the first of these were some staunch members of the Episcopal Church, whereupon Sister Smith cries out, "O, how I praise God for that grand old

' Whosoever will!' " Her fame went abroad, the country people even speaking of her with wonder and awe.

Erelong she was invited to visit Tubman Town, a point three miles distant inland from the Cape. As was her wont, she accepted this invitation and went, expecting only to spend a Sabbath. She preached in the morning, and had great liberty; the afternoon hour she spent with the children in Sabbath-school, enlightening their minds upon the subject of Gospel temperance with apparent good effect, and she regarded the prospect at Tubman Town, as well as at Mount Scott, as one of encouraging outlook.

She spoke again in the evening, and at the close of the meeting requested any that might be seeking the Lord to come forward. Five men came running to the altar, and three of them prayed their way to Calvary, and went forth with joyful hearts, praising the Lord.

For four weeks Sister Smith continued this meeting, day and night, during which twenty-five persons were brought from darkness to light, and the Lord saved them. Some of them were old men, with gray hairs, and by many had been given up as lost. Praise the Lord for this salvation! She organized female band meetings, young men's praying bands, and children's meetings for the promotion of holiness. The work was greatly blessed and owned of God.

At the end of four weeks Sister Smith returned to the Cape for a little rest. Brother Thompson, who had been placed in charge of the work there in Brother Ware's absence, asked her to conduct the Tuesday evening prayer-meeting. This she undertook to do, and the Lord so blessed her efforts that for four weeks the meetings were continued, the Lord wonderfully working with them. Speaking of these services, she says, "I gave Bible-reading lessons in the afternoon and held open-air meetings with marvelous and blessed results. The local preachers and all the official men of the Church stood by me, and we were pretty generally united in the work. Several of the local preachers and class-leaders have come into the experience of holiness. Praise the Lord! Sinners have been converted, backsliders reclaimed, and believers sanctified. To God be all the glory, for ever and ever. Amen."

Eighty persons, more or less, in Cape Palmas, and twenty-five at Tubman Town, or one hundred and five souls, brought to Christ, the Church revived, children put in a course of Christian training, backsliders reclaimed, and believers sanctified, make up the result of Sister Smith's visit to the Cape.

## HER SPECIAL MISSION TO AFRICA.

Says Sister Smith: "I believe God's leading me to Africa was that I might call the attention of the Church, both here and at home, more definitely to the subject of *holiness and Gospel temperance*. There never was a time when the attention of the Church in all lands was so clearly called to consider these subjects as in the past ten years, more or less, and why should not Africa wheel into line? May God help her!"

Sister Smith, putting her faith into words and showing it by her works, says: "I have organized bands of hope and Gospel temperance societies in all the country and towns I have visited here, except Cape Palmas and Cape Mount. I have not visited Cape Mount, and expect to organize here in Cape Palmas this week." (First week in June, 1886.)

From the work done by Sister Smith we have reports that it is making remarkable progress. For herself, she regards it as her business to work, and to trust God for results. After faithfully sowing Gospel seed, "should Israel be not gathered," she believes "Jacob will not lose his reward." So be it.

She says, "The terrible crime of intemperance has left its blasting work even in this beautiful

4

land." And this is the monument built by commerce, commemorating the effect of connection between heathen and Christian lands in trade. How long, alas! how long before enlightened Europe and America will wipe out the blasting curse of liquor-making forever?

Sister Smith, speaking of her personal condition and the effect of the climate upon her, as well as other matters pertaining to the country and people, makes the following observation:

"I am much pleased with Cape Palmas, as it is really beautiful for situation, and is considered the most healthy of all the country. For my own part, I have been better in health since I have been here than I have been in any of the other countries the same length of time, and for this I do praise the Lord; though from overwork I broke down and was laid by for two weeks, but the Lord held me up till Brother Ware got back."

It is our own opinion that Mrs. Smith's visit to Africa was a double blessing, affecting it and herself in equal measure. But it is also our belief that she has done her work there, and ought to return to bless the Churches here. Upon this point she remarks: "I am not so clear that it is the Lord's will for me to spend my days in Africa, but I am his to stay or go. Sometimes I think my work is done as far as I am able; but there is much land in this 'dark continent' yet to be possessed for God. I am glad the Lord has counted me worthy to help a little."

She is evidently thinking seriously about returning. That the evangelistic work is hers for life she does not doubt; but where the remnant of that life is to be spent is the absorbing question. Sister Smith, upon it, further says: "May God help the Church here to pray and stand fast. May he give us strength and the steadfastness to stand still and see the salvation of God. Amen. Amen." Then, thinking of her own connection with this Church and her influence upon its future, she says, "My prayer is before the Lord for light and guidance in the matter of going home or staying in Africa."

It is clear, also, that Sister Smith is willing to remain, and if needs be to suffer with her people, our people, in Africa, if that is the Lord's will.

## TOUCHING BISHOP TAYLOR'S PLANS.

Sister Smith, like all the rest of us, believes in Bishop Taylor, and in his endeavors to help the heathen to help themselves. She thinks his plans, if carried out there, will be helpful to our Liberian work. But let her speak for herself:

"I believe Bishop Taylor's plans, if carried out, for industrial schools and missions on the self-supporting principle, will be the means, under God, of solving the problem of Africa's redemption. The Grebo people are an intelligent, industrious people, natives of Cape Palmas country. The Protestant Episcopal and Methodist Episcopal Churches have done good work here years ago; but work is needed to complete that already begun. We could employ ten thousand dollars judiciously on the work here if we had it, to say nothing of Monrovia, Bassa, and Liberia. The Lord give us a baptism of real, genuine energy, and send us help."

Of our Liberia Seminary she says, "The building and site are beautiful, but in a very dilapidated condition."

How apparent is the need of a stimulus which will aid Africa! But after the expenditure of a million of dollars there, in our endeavor to develop that field, we feel sure that the stimulus, whatever it is, is not chiefly money. It is rather a spirit in the Christian men and women of Africa to help themselves; and hence Mrs. Smith's confidence in Bishop Taylor's self-supporting plans. We trust them because we believe in them, and because it is the "dernier resort."

## COMPARED TO OTHER GREAT NEGROES.

What is the place of Amanda Smith in American history? Has she any place there? Mrs. Smith is an historic character. The biography of great women, and especially of great women of the Negro race, would be sadly deficient without her.

Of this race in the United States, since 1620, there have appeared but *four* women whose career stands out so far, so high, and so clearly above all others of their sex that they can with strict propriety and upon well-established grounds be denominated *great.* These are Phillis Wheatley, Sojourner Truth, Frances Ellen Watkins Harper, and Amanda Smith.

More than a score of Negro women have arisen to heights of fame which leaped beyond the bounds of the States in which they have resided. Nor is there a single State in our country, North or South, but that could point to Negro women, a score or so in number, who are zealous of good works, endowed with a noble spirit and a love of race, sex, and self which is truly praiseworthy and distinguishing. Indeed, in every city, village, or country neighborhood, a leading Negro woman, who is a full match for its best and leading negro man, can be found.

Were this otherwise, it would present a strong incentive for melancholy, and offer some feeble extenuation to the vague and morbid dream of redemption from race degradation by race blending through blood mingling in unnatural and uncongenial amalgamation.

If there is a graduation from good to greater in the ordinary walks of female life among the Negroes, who does not feel his bosom heave with just and excusable pride when he reflects that among them are also those women who must be mentioned in the superlative, not only great, and greater, but greatest? Is there not substantial reason to hope that all may arise, when we behold one woman, then another, and another ascend from conditions the lowliest to a place freely ascribed as among the highest and the greatest?

This ascent from such a depth was made by Phillis Wheatley, Sojourner Truth, Frances Harper, and Amanda Smith.

But if these women occupy a place superlatively great as compared to all other Negro women of modern times, we would ascertain how they stand compared to each other. For it is by this comparison that we shall be able to determine which, or whether, either is greater than the other, and wherein.

To begin with, Phillis Wheatley and Sojourner Truth were both Africans of unmixed blood. Phillis Wheatley was an African of superior tribal relations by birth. Crosses in blood are sometimes found in Africa; for many traders, if no others, have a "country wife" or so while sojourning in that country. But Phillis was a child of pure Negro parentage. Mrs. Harper and Mrs. Smith were mixed in the proportion of about one part Caucasian to three parts African; hence, whatever be their claim to greatness and goodness, their racial basis for the claim is African.

Now let us compare them.

Mrs. Wheatley was the *morning star* of Negro genius, being to women what Benjamin Banneker was to Negro men, the first of her line.

Her advantages were few, and her opportunities to learn limited. But such as they were, she improved them, and secured fame as a poetess of rare pathos and beauty. Her claims as a poetess are attested by the few specimens of her verses which remain, and the claim is universally accorded to her.

An unfortunate marriage, with other disadvantages, may have interfered with the attainment of still greater renown; but as it is, Mrs. Wheatley stands peerless among American Negro women for *poetic genius*.

Sojourner Truth was a *revolutionist* and a *reformer*, with great political acumen in the rough. She was in her times the peer of Frederick Douglass, being to Negro women what he was to men. Aye, in her steadfast love to God, loyalty to the interest of all, but unyielding and undeviating fidelity, preference, and zeal for her own race, she was more than his peer.

She illustrates the capability of the race to rise by its own unaided efforts, and take a commanding and abiding place among those eminent for deeds worthy of commemoration. We have heard somewhere that the bust of Sojourner Truth adorns a place in the British Museum.

A slave born and reared, a fugitive among strangers, but not friendless there, Auntie Sojourner Truth has no equal in the display of *natural leadership* and born mental equipoise among the four great women with whom we class her.

Mrs. Harper, possessing superior advantages, is superior to any one of the four great women here mentioned in mental drill and versatile literary culture. She is an erudite, scholarly woman. She, too, is a reformer, an agitator, but not in the rough, or with any political tendencies.

She is polished, and may be called the greatest of school-made moral philosophers yet developed among the women of the Negro race. If Sojourner Truth was a blind giant, Frances Harper was an enlightened one. What she is, Sojourner, with her chances, would have been; but what Sojourner was, with no better opportunities, Mrs. Harper would never have been.

Standing outside of the Church and Churchly relations, Mrs. Harper is without an equal among Negro men of her times and type of thought. To find a literary equal for her, we must look either in the Negro ministry or among men who were trained for it.*

Mrs. Smith, in common with the others, except Mrs. Harper, came up through the enthrallments of slavery and the culture of Christian faith. She is not, then, the *scholarly agitator* that Mrs. Harper is, nor the *indomitable revolutionist* that Sojourner Truth was, nor yet the *brilliant genius* that Phillis Wheatley was. But she matches them all in this: she is a Christian of the highest type yet produced among women of her race, and as a simple, confiding child of God has no superior among women of any race—and may we modestly say it?—nor among women of any time.

She is an evangel of the Christian powers of her race, and an evangel of that good will from God to men which is the burden of her speeches.

---

* Mrs. Harper is a member of the Unitarian Church in Philadelphia, and stands high in it, I learn.—AUTHOR.

As a demonstration of the possibilities of the Negro woman—and if the woman, then also the man—to grasp and hold a place among those who have attained the highest heights of Christian faith and perfect self-consecration to the service of God and man, Amanda Smith stands without a rival.

Without the genius of Mrs. Wheatley, the daring of Sojourner Truth, the logic of Mrs. Harper, Mrs. Smith has a greatness born not of self nor of mind, but of *soul culture* by contact with God. Herein is she great, the equal of either, and greater than any. Among men of our race and times, none equal Mrs. Smith as exemplifiers of the power of grace to save, expand, and use man as an instrumentality of salvation to the human race.

She is in these particulars, then, as we have frequently said, not only the greatest Negro woman, but the greatest of the race in these times.

Let Negro women study well her character and imitate it. Let them read well her struggle up from sin and Satan to God, and use the same means, if they, too, would rise like her in his likeness and image.

What grace has wrought in her it has wrought for our ensample, that like her in use of means at hand, so like her we afterwards might be useful in the Master's hands.

As an enlightened, thoroughly consecrated Christian evangelist, among Negro women, Mrs. Amanda Smith takes the first place in American history.

# ACKNOWLEDGMENT.

EARLY in August, 1886, through the SOUTH-WESTERN CHRISTIAN ADVOCATE, we solicited the friends of Sister Amanda Smith, then in Cape Palmas, Liberia, West Coast of Africa, for a donation in small sums, which, including one pound sterling ($4.85), paid by Sister Smith herself, would be equal to the aggregate amount of $9.52.

In response to this solicitation we received the various amounts from the parties to whom they are herein credited, making a total of $15.57, being $6.05 above the amount required.

It was our purpose to apply this fund, in accordance with the desire of Sister Smith, to the payment of one year's subscription to the SOUTHWESTERN CHRISTIAN ADVOCATE, $1.52; then $8 was to be used in making an engraving, and in preparing a sketch of Sister Smith for newspaper use, and the remainder, $6.05, was, according to our promise, to be held subject to Sister Smith's order.

But when the work was all ready for print there was a good-sized volume of it, too much to print at

one time with the large type we use in our paper.
To have printed it in serial form would have spoiled
it, and it was too precious for condensation. What
must be done? I believe the Spirit of the Lord gave
the answer, Publish it in book form. When the path
of duty is plain, conviction with us means action.
Hence this publication.

But there was the money sent us by Sister Smith
and her friends. It was far short of enough to put
the matter in its present shape. I was not at liberty
to use it otherwise than as stated in the appeal, and
therefore concluded to pay Sister Smith the entire
amount of $15.67, less $1.52, the subscription price
of the SOUTHWESTERN, plus postage, to her one year.
I have accordingly placed to the credit and at the
disposal of Sister Smith $14.05, for all of which, on
her and my own behalf, I make very grateful ac-
knowledgments to the givers. The Lord bless and
increase them every one a thousand-fold.

## CONTRIBUTORS AND CREDITS.

Amount required, . . . . . . . . . . . . . . . . . $9 52
Credit on same by foreign draft from Mrs. Amanda
      Smith, one pound sterling, . . . . . . . . . 4 85

**BY WHITE FRIENDS.**
      Rev. D. P. Kidder, D. D., New York, . . . . 4 00
      Mrs. Mary A. Carley, Kentucky, . . . . . . 2 00
      Rev. J. H. Vincent, D. D., New York, . . . . 1 00

**BY COLORED FRIENDS.**
      Rev. W. S. McMillan, Texas, . . . . . . . . 1 00
      Mrs. Kate Taylor, Louisiana, . . . . . . . . 25

Rev. W. H. Evans, Kentucky, . . . . . . . $0 25
Miss Alice Young, Louisiana, . . . . . . . . 25
In behalf of the Indiana District, Lexington
    Methodist Episcopal Conference, by
Rev. Charles Jones, P. E., Indiana, . . . . . 50
Rev. A. A. Price, Indiana, . . . . . . . . . 25
Rev. S. G. Turner, Indiana, . . . . . . . . . 25
Rev. C. T. Jones, Indiana, . . . . . . . . . 25
Rev. Frederick White, Indiana, . . . . . . . 25
Rev. D. W. Heston, Indiana, . . . . . . . . 15
Rev. Frank Hinton, Indiana, . . . . . . . . 12
Rev. W. B. Harris, Indiana, . . . . . . . . . 10
Rev. J. B. Collins, Indiana, . . . . . . . . . 10

Total, . . . . . . . . . . . . . . . . $15 57
Amount required, . . . . . . . . . . . . . . . . 1 52

Balance in hand subject to Mrs. Smith's order, . . $14 05

Respectfully and thankfully,

MARSHALL W. TAYLOR.

# ►HOW TO GET IT!◄

# THE LIFE, TRAVELS, & LABORS

#### — OF —

# MRS. AMANDA SMITH,

## The Negro Missionary and Evangelist.

#### ILLUSTRATED. PRICE, 25 CENTS CASH.

### BY

# MARSHALL W. TAYLOR, D. D.,

*Editor of the Southwestern Christian Advocate; Author of the " Life of Rev. G. W. Downing;" and Compiler of " Plantation Melodies," etc.*

MRS. SMITH has traveled and preached in America, England, Scotland, Ireland, India, and Africa. She has been borne along upon a tidal wave of grace, and under God has greatly aided in exemplifying the holiness she professes.

The Story is worthy of a careful perusal, and we commend it to all, especially to women. It makes a neat present to a Christian friend.

Address orders to

## CRANSTON & STOWE,

### 190 West Fourth Street,
#### CINCINNATI, O.

www.ingramcontent.com/pod-product-compliance
Lightning Source LLC
Chambersburg PA
CBHW020519030426
42337CB00011B/459